THE ICE BENEATH THE EARTH

BRIAN ASCALON ROLEY
POEMS

C&R Press
Conscious & Responsible

C&R Press
Conscious & Responsible
crpress.org

For special discounted bulk purchases, please contact:
C&R Press sales@crpress.org
Contact info@crpress.org to book events, readings and author signings.

THE ICE BENEATH THE EARTH

For my family, with gratitude

TABLE OF CONTENTS

FISHERMEN

I. CORAL REEF

Kawayan. In summer
the minus tide brought out the coral reef
exposed, bone-white in moonlight
we walked out barefoot
scouted for crabs, baby octopi
sea urchin you could break open
to harvest the soft marrow parts
the maids could cook up
to eat. Inay feared
feet lacerations.
Uncut I came away
half leg
jellyfished
to burn
clutching my knee
screaming it hurts into the arms
of the laughing yayas
and their soothing
                        balms.

II. DOGFIGHTS

These same beaches, years before
saw Japanese and American war planes
dogfight over the skies.
Our inay and her brothers
used to watch from that cliff
above the bay
the planes' shadows
play tag, wander
flicker and dart over the beach
across the bay bottom
out to the submerged coral reef.

One time, a plane crashed
out on that reef, half-submerged;
her brothers tossed off their shirts
—Betino and Pepe both—
and swam out to investigate
whether the pilot was worth saving.

They disappeared into the blinding
sea-shimmer, their mother berating her men
for letting them go, pacing the sand
in her Spanish dress, embroidered
down to her calves
brushing beach that powdered her ankles
like chalk.

She squinted, they returned a blur
out of the water.
Was he alive? Tio Salvador asked.
Yes.
Japanese or Amerikanos?

BRIAN ASCALON ROLEY

Pepe, the shy one, looked down
at his feet. Betino stepped forward
and told him Japanese.
Tio Salvador grunted, spat at the foaming
water that sizzled into wet sand
took off his own shirt
and leapt out into the sea-coruscation.

III. AFTER THE WAR
Voice of Dina

After the war some soldiers did not hear
that their Emperor had surrendered
in Japan
and so hid out in the jungles, eating
insects and roots and even monkeys, people said
our guerrilla uncles would go out hunting
for them like boars
brought back their heads
staked on bamboo sticks
through rowdy village crowds until, as with boars,
none were left.

One afternoon a typhoon blew in
from the north and cleared
revealed a fishing boat
apparently drifted down from Japan
to these waters near Navarro bay;
village boys came calling
out to us, through hurried breaths,
said they'd spotted her
anchoring, already laying nets.
Salvador and his men
went out and put fire to the boat.
That night we could see it flame
on the black ocean, coughing up
red spark clouds to the pagan constellations.

BRIAN ASCALON ROLEY

What happened to the Japanese fishermen?
my sister interrupted. Inay turned away from Ate,
refused to answer but we followed
her into the kitchen and persisted
until Inay turned off the faucet, threw up her hands
and complied.

But they were just innocents!
Ate shouted. Inay shrugged, After
the war, people were very angry.

What did the Japanese do to make
them so pissed off? I asked.

Inay took notice of me, pursed
her lips and said, Let this be a lesson,
my darlings. People do not forget
slights no matter how easily
you may have given them.
It does not matter if you think
they are not worth remembering.

IV. FISHERMEN

Jesus was a fisherman, Ate protested.
Hindi, Inay snapped. You have it wrong.
That was Simon and Andrew and Peter. Jesus walked
on water.

V. PIRATA

Now, Salvador is an old
man, though his rock-hard arms
still pop veins
as he shades his eyes and squints
at a small vessel
out on our bay.
Pirata, he says
with a poker face.
Inay's hand tightens
in mine.

Pirata, he calls them.
Three thin men, so wishbone slight
as they paddle
their simple kayak of a boat—a bangka—
they appear to vanish
within the firmament.

Fishermen, Inay explains
once we are out of Salvador's
earshot. Cyanide and dynamite
equipped, they float into our bay
on their little bangka with outriggers
of hollowed bamboo, toss their poison
into waters, pick up the floating bloated spoils,
then hurry off to prepare them for market.

The reef, she is sick,
Lolo Salvador says
as we motor over
the white skeleton
shining up at us with
blackened marks
a gap
like a bite in its side
the shape of an enormous arrowhead.

VI. KAWAYAN MARKET

We bite into the white fish
bought at Kawayan market
salt of sea on the tongue, tamarin
squeezed into the broth
and something faint, perhaps
a spice imagined
or what I imagine might taste
like cyanide.
A small girl child watches me
from her family's table
sideways as she bites into
her own
piece of Philippine ocean.

This taste on my tongue, like fine sand,
salty, granular, dust.

VII. THE OLD GUERRILLA

1

A child vomits and takes to her bed
with fever. We bring a healer to her
nipa hut. Something is in the air,
from the corner, musty. The woman dabs
at the sleeping girl's forehead with a white cloth,
her eyes worried. She turns to the hovering
mother. What did she eat?
Fish at Kawayan, the woman says,
and the albularyo shakes her head.

I wander about that afternoon in the mango
orchard, fallen fruit fetid in the sun, holding my gut
imagining organ aches and frowning until I look up
to see the old guerrilla watching me; I blush
and stand straight, untouch my stomach.
He turns to his foreman. We must protect
the children, he says.

2

The old guerrilla gathers his kumpadres
at fiesta dance that night,
his barrel-chested nephews,
a dozen village men in army pants,
camouflage t-shirts, Tagalog barongs,
examining automatic rifles, grenades,
pistols leftover from various rebellions
and wars. Some have fought Moros
in Mindanao, flown helicopters in Korea
or Vietnam, ambushed Marcos's soldiers,
Americans, Japanese. Some were Maoists
who tried to take Salvador's land and failed,
yet live still though others died.
But now they love the old guerrilla, his stories and gin.
They plan patrols on the bay in motorboats
armed with sleek descendants of the Gatling gun.
For the children, he toasts with a shot glass, to many nods.
Tiny children go out onto the village square
to dance. So beautiful, our Tita says to us
in our corner, her voice lightly accented
from years in Germany where she left
a husband and three grown children behind.
These tiny darlings will be married
within a decade. Virgins still.

VIII. BARANGAY FIESTA

Food again. All we do
here is eat, we say. Don't complain
in front of these people, Inay snaps. You
American children don't know how lucky
you are. Ate says: Oh please.
The pig whose cries squealed
throughout the valley as it waited
to be slaughtered
this morning
(tied by noose
to a coconut tree, which dug rope
burns into her neck because she tugged so hard,
her companion wailing just steps away, on a picnic
table, pinned belly-down by three peasants as a man slit
her throat above a dripping pail
to catch blood falling, a delicacy
and another climbed on its chest, stood above
the heart
to push it all out
the pig's eyes weakening as she looked at me, pleading
intelligent,
her screams become softer, almost
a whisper)
comes out now on paper plates
roasted, fresh, pieces of gelatinous fat
glistening against crisp
skin and feels soft
in the mouth.

IX. LAST HAPUNAN ["Kagiliwan"]

1

What can I tell you about the fishermen?
Three gaunt men, coral-killers, child-poisoners,
trespassers who take from nature
hungry, near-starved, jobless, landless,
no doubt fathers all.

2

Word would come to us about the bangka
pirata, three burnt bodies found entangled
down shore, among mangroves
emaciated, sodden, crab-climbed
bits of their blackened boat-wood
floating in stagnant pools
of minus tide.

Four young policia arrive
from Kawayan, men whom you'd expect
to arrest Lolo Salvador for pagpatay
but who sit with him and drink
at the men's picnic table
in the shade of the acacia tree
instead, sharing stories and San Miguel beer
kept in a bottle crate at his feet

replenished always by scurrying
girls. I sit at the women's table
nearby, embarrassed
not to be with the men. Inay stares
at her plate looking sad
too sick
to eat
but my aunt feeds us
fresh crab and adobo
sliced pre-ripe mango with dipping salt.
Those lazy men
sell the fish with cyanide to mothers
and children at market, our aunt
says to our mother. Don't
feel sad for them.

Inay flinches at the sound
of laughter coming from the men's
table. Tita watches Inay's untouched plate,
shakes her head and says, You've been in California
too long, cousin. Jumping to conclusions
about things you cannot understand.
For all we know it was their own dynamite
that killed them. She clucks her tongue.
You've forgotten
how fresh seafood tastes.
Learn from your son, so Filipino
watch how he eats
with such lovely appetite!

She smiles at me.
The fresh crab caught in our bay
this morning feels in my mouth
like a recently living thing.
From somewhere in a jungle valley
comes a distant sound, a scream
or squeal, perhaps imagined, faint.

18   BRIAN ASCALON ROLEY

SPITFIRE ["Why Did Sir Robert McLean Name a
Murderous Warplane After His Favorite Daughter?"]

1

Words related: wench, fury, siren, hussy, bitch, hellion
nag, scold, battle-axe

2

Strange to give the nickname of your beloved
daughter to a warplane that can bring bullets
and noise to you in such a violent hurry,
to imbed you with that flush of injury
and acute accumulation of pain.

Perhaps the knighted Scotsman envisioned dead
Germans' stratified bodies
upon the fields of Saxony, the plains of Bavaria,
the ancient streets of Dresden
when he penned the name of the murderous
aircraft.

However, I prefer to think he got satisfaction
from imagining his daughter's future suitors
being taken down a notch
by her vivacious barbs
kept from getting too large a head
even as her father declined
inevitably into old age and dottery.

Strange to think how some imaginings
can give us satisfaction.

3

My mother recalls a dogfight
her family watched from a soccer
match in Quezon Provence, Japanese and American
warplanes rumbling low over mountains
to the east, coming like a wall
of typhoon rain
their sound first, deafening
as turbines.
She recalls the glint of sun spark
on fuselage, wing or glass
then metal bellies
drifting over the musty crowd like the undersides
of clouds or sharks,
as they all cheered for the American
to hit his target
and Japanese officers watched
from the best seats in the stadium
their place of honor.

EXPOSURES

They say we should not expose
you to too much heat or sun
bright, that your body may lose
homeostasis
and go into multiple organ
failure
due to the mitochondrial
                         disease

that at the slightest sign of fever or
dehydration, we need
to take you to an emergency
room for an IV
drip of glucose infusion

a piece of advice we did not obey
one Christmas Eve in California
despite your vomiting
due to news reports
emergency rooms were full
of flu and fever and bacteria-
carrying crowds that winter

only to be rebuked by Dr Wendy Wu
back in Ohio
who sat down opposite us and looked
at my wife in particular
and said,
In case you do not understand—mom and dad
your boy could easily lose his heart, kidneys,
liver, sight and die
so do not do that again

A PARTNER'S SECRET

She did not know that in childhood
I spoke with a speech impediment.

These days my students bring in notes
inform me they have hidden or not so hidden
disabilities
for which they are entitled
accommodations they discuss openly
to the class.

But my childhood occupied
a different time. High school
classmates put an autistic girl in a trash
can with impunity, and teased a deaf boy
relentlessly in front of hippie teachers.
Back then a stutter
was something my psychology
professor (who wrote the famous textbook)
made fun of while I sat silent
in a Wesleyan auditorium
and the artsy girl next to me
laughed so hard she cried.

At 17, I learned my uncle once had one
too. My father confided in me as we
left the theater after watching Michael Palin
tormented by the actor everybody loved, Kevin
Kline, to the Westwood audience's delight
and I blushed
realizing that Dad had noticed
that I'd laughed too

when Palin had to swallow his beloved pet
fish because he could not utter
proper words.

TONGUES

Despite his command of the language, Nabokov regretted
not knowing English as a first tongue, yearned
for a native's sensitivity to nuance. My Cornell
professor insisted his migration allowed the Russian great
his fecundity of wordplay. But Nabokov made me sad
not to be able to read Anna Karenina in Cyrillic.

Our 19th c. poet-martyr,
Jose Rizal, befriended linguists in Europe
so he could catalogue the many languages
of the Philippines, which he feared would be lost.
A polymath, he spoke several handfuls
of languages.
European women of background fell in love
with him despite his brown skin, short stature,
colonial status. I suppose it's a good
thing my ancestors threw off
the Spanish yoke, at times violently

but I wish I could hear the poetry
of Rizal in Spanish with the same ear
for its nuances as might a goat herder
from Andalusia
or perhaps a Russian peasant hearing War
and Peace sung to them in the time
of Tolstoy.

BRIAN ASCALON ROLEY

TACTICS ["Anting-anting"]

During the last decades of the Spanish empire
revolutionary leader Emilio Aguinaldo
popularized the practice of posting heads
of native collaborators along roadsides
as warning to behave.
After the Amerikanos allies betrayed
him and took his country as their own
that decorative practice continued

among others that would be studied
across decades and continents—by Vietcong,
Castro, FARC, Peshmerga, Mujahideen
—and taught
at U.S. military colleges into the present century.

In our new schools in California
we did not learn about Aguinaldo's ambush
nor of the half century of U.S. colonial
rule that followed, though we did spend
several weeks studying about European acquisitions
and their not-so-best-practices in
Latin America, India, Africa,
Bora Bora, Tahiti, the Middle East.

Why do you Filipinos speak
such good English?
our schoolmates asked.

Aguinaldo was said to have
anting-anting—the mystic
power
to evade your bullets or capture
but the Amerikanos eventually did fell
him by arranging a fake parley
under white flag
and attacking the men
and their horses
a practice Lt Funston learned from men
who in boyhood hunted the last great
warriors of the arid plains,
Comancheria
and remembered.

BRIAN ASCALON ROLEY

ACCENTS

When we used to go to the coconut farm out
in Quezon province, my mother and her cousins
could not understand the locals, said they spoke
"deep" Tagalog, which made them giggle
to hear, and the peasants smiled broadly,
apparently pleased.

In high school we embarked upon a trip
to the nation's capital, pooled with a hundred pupils
from parochial Dallas schools. They said y'all
and laughed at the way we spoke with such
heavy accents, coming from the coast of California.

When my wife moved to Chicago in late high school
her new classmates laughed at her
Texas accent, at her drawls and spark, though she insists
it was imparted with affection.

My wife no longer speaks like a Texan, said she lost
it over a couple years of trying to fit in,
which I think is a shame. She says, "Well, I'll pick
it back up if we move to Texas, something I'd love."

I say, "Now when I have students from Texas, they sound
just like any kid from suburban Ohio. So I wouldn't be so sure."

We greeted my mother at the airport, on her return
from the Philippines. She looked happy, shared all the tsissmis
over merienda past midnight. But Inay said when she traveled
out to the country, the magsasaka all talk now like people
do in Manila. "I can actually understand them," she said.

"Well, that must be a good thing, right?" my wife said.

Inay looked at her a bit sadly, pondered it, and shrugged.
"You would think so. People should be able to communicate."

When my grandmother left Laguna for the Visayan island
where her new husband, my grandfather, came from
they spoke to each other in Spanish because neither
knew each other's dialects. She marveled, in a Castilian accent,
at how few Virgins people possessed, preferring Infant
of Pragues carved of expensive molave wood and imbedded
with jewels. "We love children here, more than mothers," his
mother said.

AFTER THE OCCUPATION ["Makati Hilton 1992"]

1

In the Makati hospital slotted glass
lets in the smog damp air of Manila.
You can walk in off the street
and if you look like you know
what you are doing
nobody will stop you.
The crowd flows in off the crowded
sidewalk, into the lobby, up the stairs.
People cram halls and smokers stand shoulder
to shoulder on the rooftop, just outside
the cafeteria's open doors.

We saw a sooty, sweat-shriveled mouse
scamper by the waiter's shoes.

2

Because nurses let relatives of a comatose
girl serve food and wine to visiting guests,
the halls of the ICU smell of soy sauce,
bay leaf and moist pork adobo. They cook
on a kerosene camp stove on the floor
just outside my lola's sheet partition.

Inside, a relative boy runs
about without a germ-mask coughing
over my lola whose respirator tube
sticks out of her cut-open throat.
Ate stares at this boy cousin evilly
and goes up to our mother and says, "Get him out
of here, or make him wear a mask."

"Hush!" Inay snaps, with a mortified
look at the boy's mother, because she does not want
us to be impolite.

3

"It'll kill her, do you want to see
your own mother die?"
Ate asks and our mother turns
aside, as if she cannot
hear us or understand.

4

The cough-boy's mother, Inay's younger cousin of 26,
glances bitterly at Ate, lips pursed tight.

5

Your sister looks Spanish, our cousins tell me.
Just like those lovely mestisa bitches
at school, but not stuck up.
But she acts American. You though,
look American.

6

"Back in my school in Los Angeles, I was called gook, flat face,
chink eye, slant eye, jungle n_____r. A kid threw a fist
into my stomach on the tag football field and said
it was for his uncle who died in Vietnam.

American soldiers coined the term gook in the jungles of Luzon
when they took the Philippines during the aftermath of the
Spanish American War

then at home I clutched my gut and told Inay I had poisoning
from food at school, stared at my eyes in the mirror, red now
with crusted salt, and lay in bed under a sheet."

7

Last week we killed a winged cockroach
on the ICU ceiling the size of a bat.
My titas snuck in a giant faith-healing nun.
She shimmered in an electric blue habit,
towering next to her twelve-year-old cowering
girl assistant, and insisted we feed her first
at a pricy restaurant.

"I need nourishment to heal," she snorted.
"And if anybody is present who does not believe,
it will make me very angry."

Ate looked at me and pulled a face, then left the room.

8

Afterward she touched our chests and foreheads and people fell
to the ground.
     I felt electric, burning, a concussive light.
     When I stood, I felt a bruising, swelling on my chest in
the shape of a fist.

I still feel a bruise there now.

9

Down in Subic Bay the Americans dismantle their base,
like naughty husbands sent packing.
Our local relatives who seem to have decided
my sister looks Spanish do not worry about her
feeling hurt, but glance at me
and my white father with concern.
My tita shakes her head and faces him:
"It's foolish, Wade. We need your money
and protection. These Manila politicians
with their fake nationalism should not be
so touchy. Jesus says there is sin in pride."

10

Lola writes on her pad to the pulmonary specialist, "You are
handsome. You must have three wives."
    He laughs, strokes her cheek, smiles into her eyes, gently
thumbs her earlobe.
    She looks up at him like a frail child.
    In the hall light he takes us aside. Faces Inay.
    "It has come to occupy your mother."
    "It?" Inay says.
    He takes both her hands.
    "It happens. Sometimes one kind, she will enter first, and
make the host ready for the other. The pneumonia left your inay,
but tuberculosis occupied her place."
    Our mother begins to tremble.
    "How do we get it out of her!" my sister says, stroking
and supporting Inay's elbow.
    The surgeon appears surprised to be addressed by a girl
so, then pulls her into a hug.

11

On the highways outside people may sometimes lay like roadkill
as drivers pass without pausing, but in the home among kin and
kumpadre they touch you without fear.

Rich people and foreigners call
this place the Makati Hilton
but Ate calls it a third world hospital.
Our white father sits
on the wood bench outside Lola's room
looking tired from smiling
at his wife's relatives
and stares out the window
now, at the typhoon rains that come
in at a slant and rattle the walls
leak in through the cracks
and touch his face.

THE ICE BENEATH THE EARTH

The ice beneath the earth
is what she told us to watch
out for, something you could feel
beneath bare feet, through frozen
grass. That was long ago
when her voice carried far
chasing us through leafless woods
of pine and aspen
when Ashton and Tabitha and I
hid in our makeshift forts
beween teepeed branches
huddled and willing ourselves
not to be found
by mothers. I can't remember why
we did this and actually
had not thought of either one in years
so the jolt of it yesterday
caught me
when I saw her name in the newspaper
caption, beneath the picture of an adult
woman I did not recognize
shrouded as she was by a fleshy mask of middle age.
Then came that sudden ghost apprehension
that caught my breath
how she was decades ago
all at once unearthed
from early childhood to high school parting
what had apparently been there all these ages
unseen, this lovely girl in her becoming
something the man beside her
in the picture would never
know.

BRIAN ASCALON ROLEY

APOLOGY

sometimes it is hard to drink
orange juice when your throat muscles
are weak, and to walk
without hip strength or even
to sit up and balance
without mid-torso support

when hot moist rooms
can make your legs wobble
even simple sunlight, so cheering
to others can make you wither
on those legs

but often what's worse is thinking
about your caregiver
pushing your wheelchair through crowds
and you looking back up at her face

as she strains to maneuver
you down the awkward pebbled path
between restaurant chairs your feet need
to bump, through narrow
aircraft aisles and all those protruding elbows
purses, fingers

she offers nervous smiles
to people who need
to move their knuckles or feet
the bottlenecked crowd irritated
behind her, whispers gathering
and on her face
a girlish blush

you could only call beautiful
she touches her hair
your mother
as if she heard something there
she wants to hide.

BRIAN ASCALON ROLEY

ASSEMBLAGES

She built you a makeshift
beach wheelchair, sand friendly
with pvc piping and huge plastic tires
that float on water
like Christ

so that you can smell the salt, feel the icy
splash on your ankles, achilles, calves
while your brother leaps
into crowded waves

THESE DAYS SHE IS VIGILANT

with sunhats and mobile fans, will not
take you into cars without aircon on a hot summer
day

so how will I ever bring you to the Philippines
that country full of heat and germs
yet also kin enchanted
titas who sing tsissmis as they feed
you laughing just to see you eat,
who cherish lucky children
as you will be for not much longer? I often promised

I'd give you the memory
of your Lola Dina's country in childhood
as I'd been given
to take with you into adulthood
as we keep memories of loved
ones tucked close
after they are gone: scent of my grandfather's
sugarcane rattling in salt winds of the Visayan ocean.
Taste of fresh crabs
picked on Tita's coral reef at low tide.
The pre-dawn trek among crowds in darkness
to nine days of Christmas mass amid the smell of nipa
thatch and rosemary ash and sweat.
Loud rush of water coursing through Manila streets
while Tito's metal rooftop is pelted by typhoon
rain muted to a lyric patter
by which you can fall into the sleep
finally, to which you've always been so terrified
of succumbing.

TITHE ["Tito Above Our Garage"]

She ran her finger over the car's silver
paint and felt the residue of dust
soot and pollen, the moment she realized
he had been cleaning their cars
these years
in secret of early morning dark.
This brother who had lived his adult
years above her garage,
first as caretaker for their mother, later
elderly himself.

This is how it will hit you
they are gone: when the gutters clog
with leaves and water leaks into your husband's
office; when you return to the airport
and his rusty old car isn't at the curb;
when you open the kitchen closet to find
empty shelves, because you are afraid
to go to Costco during these times
of plague whereas he, aged 89, was not.

We live in an age of boasting, talk,
posting. Tito was not a brand,
this uncle lived above our garage caretaking
his mother until she died, then stayed
the remainder of his life.
When my mother tried to throw
him a birthday party, he'd see cars
at the curb and turn around, drive away.
The Pharisees argued they deserved
the front seats in the Temple; the widow
gave her last coin
not for status.
RIP Nonoy.

MIGRATION ["Carabao"]

At school we learned of the Caribou
migrations, great herds thundering
across continents, over frozen grass
sedges, forbs, scrubs chased by calculating packs
of nimble wolves.

But my mind filled with visions
of the Philippine carabao
black, big-horned, lumbering beast
slow, stubborn, of ox-strong haunches, nostrils
flared and angry.
I could not comprehend how such a thick-boned

monster could migrate so many miles, across oceans.
How could this water buffalo used to wading
tropic swamps prance across tundra
like ballerina to outrun wolves? How did they swim
from an island nation to the cold country
up north? Why would they flee the warm swamp
jungles where they could eat all day
lazily in rivers,
why swap such languid Eden for barren
plains beneath silvery skies?

Like my mother's own migration
decades ago, bewildering.
She came from a country full of crowded
streets and bedrooms, homes full of eating
guests and tita laughter
nephews who dote on elders without
embarrassment,
to this country of cold winters, wide lawns,
where her inlaws don't even know the names
of second cousins
and teenage kin shelter
behind closed bedroom doors
at the sight of her coming
and nobody offers guests leftovers
after parties
in case they might wake up lonely
the taste of something imagined
on their tongues.

BRIAN ASCALON ROLEY

REFUGEES

My son interviewed my father for a school
project about adversity, in which he needed
to draw affinities to a book about Vietnamese
boat people and what hardships
they had to overcome.

He could have picked my mother, brown-skinned
so impoverished during the Japanese
occupation they shared a single egg among seven cousins,
watched relatives slaughtered like pigs
planes shot down screaming from the sky.
                              But he'd heard

stories of my neglected father, white-skinned,
unsung, from cornfield and factory country. Knew my father
lived in an uncle's bar in childhood, brushed his teeth in the metal
sink, slept on a cot behind a curtain
as grown men shot pool,
and grownups danced
to juke boxes. He showered at gym
class, worked fields in humid summers
bailed hay, poured hot highway tar that filled his lungs
and perhaps gave him the disease which has come to
take his life. He was the first in his family to go to college,
migrate to California, then risk everything by chucking
his safe ledgering job to start a business.

Yet my father surprised him, spoke instead
about an old speech impediment
my son did not know about. People would talk
and he'd not be able to get a word out
before they continued on, which was embarrassing, and worse
they'd grow nervous and jump in with more words
which can make childhood feel like an endless conversation
in which you can never keep up.

My son, who like me has his own struggles speaking,
listened intently from his wheelchair, eyes on the Skype screen
as my father told him about becoming college class president
among a student body of thousands, giving speeches
to large auditoriums for work, managing groups of spitfire
salesmen. Thirty minutes later
Dad still talked, my son raptly watching, noticing
that my father, despite a bit of coughing
from the disease that tries to exhaust his lungs,
had never reached for his oxygen tank
had not tripped up on a single word
in recounting his life's story
and seemed in no mood to stop.

1521 ["Imposter Prince"]

The guidebooks tell you that Santo Nino
is just a local name for the Infant of Prague.
My grandmother had one in her
back alley room, which I would visit
when angry at Inay, to sit with her and pray
beneath the crowned baby's wooden feet
she so adored
forehead flickering by votive candleflame.

I go back to find it, decades later, within the closet
pile of her old belongings, mostly junk
my mother did not have the cojones to sort
and toss. Sweaters threadbare or tattered
by moths; old tins of Filipino candies
brought home in balikbayan boxes
whose cardboard walls fray
apart in my hands, the must bursting
out to fill my nostrils with something moldy
like old cheese unwrapped
at market, the seller telling you, Go on, eat.
It's supposed to taste that way.
And the crowned baby looking up at you,
in your hand
         the wood dry rot cracked
costume jewels however resplendent
protected from the sun
these years

now unhidden by my hands, birthed
from the adoring clutch of my lola's sweaters
into a world unprotected.

This is what the Queen of Cebu saw!
unveiled by arriving conquistadors
so lovely it made her kneel
at his feet
she who named him Santo Nino
in sight of the first explorer, still gaunt
from his journey across two oceans, teeth worn
from chewing rat meat and Spanish leather.
This is 1521,
three decades before the birth
of that other boy whom the sisters cloak
in the Discalced Carmelite Church
of Our Lady Victorious
half our earth away.
This, the year Magellan died.

BRIAN ASCALON ROLEY

ACKNOWLEDGEMENTS

"After the Occupation" originally appeared in *The Iowa Review*. "A Partner's Secret" and "Refugees" appeared in *Intima: A Journal of Narrative Medicine*. "Apology" appeared in *The Columbia Poetry Review*. "Migrations ['Carabao']" and "Tactics" appeared in *For a Better World 2023, Poems and Drawings on Peace and Justice*, ed. Saad Ghosn, SOS Art Cincinnati, 2023 (also paired with visual art and exhibited at The Annex Gallery, Pendleton Art Center, Cincinnati, 2023). My deepest gratitude goes out to all the editors and poets who have given me advice on these and other poems, including my students and family, and the editors and staff of C & R Press.

ABOUT THE AUTHOR

Brian Ascalon Roley is a writer and professor of Philippine and American descent. A recent National Endowment of the Arts Literature Fellow, he is Professor of English and Director of Creative Writing at Miami University.

He has held additional fellowships, research appointments and residencies from the University of Cambridge, Cornell University, the Ohio Arts Council, Djerassi, Ragdale, the VCCA, and others. His short works in several genres (Fiction, Poetry, CNF and Hybrid) have appeared in many prestigious journals and in anthologies from Norton and Penguin, as well as several best selling anthologies in the Philippines. His works include *American Son* (WW Norton), *The Last Mistress of Jose Rizal* (Northwestern UP), and *Ambuscade* (FLP Open Chapbook Competition Prize). Learn more about the author at brianroley.com.

BRIAN ASCALON ROLEY

C&R PRESS CHAPBOOKS

C&R Press hosts two chapbook selection periods from June to September and November to March each year. The Summer Tide Pool and Winter Soup Bowl Chapbook Series are open to new and established writers in poetry, fiction, essay and other creative writing genres.

2023 SUMMER TIDE POOL
The Consolation of Geometry by Alice Campbell Romano

2023 WINTER SOUP BOWL
Allison A. deFreese's translation from Spanish of Luciana Jazmín Coronado's *Dinner at Las Heras*

2022 SUMMER TIDE POOL
The Ice Beneath the Earth by Brian Ascalon Roley

2022 WINTER SOUP BOWL
tommy noun by Maurya Kerr

2021 SUMMER TIDE POOL
Rocketflower by Matthew Meade

2021 WINTER SOUP BOWL
We Face the Tremenedous Meat on the Teppan by Naoko Fujimoto

2020 WINTER SOUP BOWL
My Roberto Clemente by Rick Hilles

2019 SUMMER TIDE POOL
Inside the Orb of an Oracle by Dannie Ruth

2019 WINTER SOUP BOWL
The Magical Negro Reveals His Secret by Gabriel Green

2018 SUMMER TIDE POOL
Yell by Sarah Sousa

2018 WINTER SOUP BOWL
Paleotemptestology by Bertha Crombet

White Boys from Hell by Jeffrey Skinner

2017 SUMMER TIDE POOL
Atypical Cells of Undetermined Significance by Brenna Womer

2017 WINTER SOUP BOWL
Heredity and Other Inventions by Sharona Muir

On Inaccuracy by Joe Manning

2016 SUMMER TIDE POOL
Cuntstruck by Kate Northrop

Relief Map by Erin M. Bertram

Love Undefined by Jonathan Katz

2016 WINTER SOUP BOWL
Notes from the Negro Side of the Moon by Earl Braggs

A Hunger Called Music: A Verse History in Black Music
  by Meredith Nnoka